Watson Griffin

The Provinces and the States

Why Canada does not want Annexation

Watson Griffin

The Provinces and the States
Why Canada does not want Annexation

ISBN/EAN: 9783337209483

Printed in Europe, USA, Canada, Australia, Japan

Cover: Foto ©ninafisch / pixelio.de

More available books at **www.hansebooks.com**

THE PROVINCES

AND

THE STATES

WHY CANADA DOES NOT WANT ANNEXATION

BY

WATSON GRIFFIN

———————————

TORONTO

J. MOORE, PUBLISHER, 39 COLBORNE ST.

1884

The Provinces and the States

SEVERAL of the leading American and English magazines have lately published articles setting forth the supposed advantages that the Canadian provinces would secure by annexation to the United States. Canada has nothing to gain by annexation. I will not deny that the material progress of the provinces would have been far greater had they joined the great republic one hundred years ago, but it does not follow that they would be benefitted by the adoption of such a course to-day, for while obtaining none of the advantages which an early union would have assured they would become subject to many evils resulting from the past mistakes of the American people.

In instituting comparisons between the provinces and the states, it is necessary to bear in mind the fact that Canada, as now

constituted, is only seventeen years old. Prior
to 1867 the provinces were not united and had
no general policy. Each province had to compete, not only with the states taken individu-
ally, but with the states collectively. It was
not Ontario or Nova Scotia against Michigan
or Maine, but Ontario or Nova Scotia against
the United States of America. The position
is different now. It is the Dominion of Canada,
extending from the Atlantic to the Pacific,
against the United States alongside. Mani-
festly the comparative progress of the two
countries in the past is no indication of their
relative position in this regard in the future.

Had the Canadian provinces confederated
fifty years ago and adopted a national policy
for the encouragement of interprovincial trade,
the rapid settlement of Ontario would have
aided in the development of the eastern provinces. For half a century the people of the
eastern states have been migrating to the
west, but the Yankees have not suffered from
the exodus because the migrants were still
under the same general government, and being
unable at first to supply themselves with
manufactured goods, were obliged by the tariff
to purchase from the manufacturers of the

eastern states. Horace Greeley's injunction, " Go west, young man !" operated as strongly on the mind of the young Canadian as it did on that of the young American, but Canada had no west, and so thousands left the country to push their fortunes in the western states. The provinces were disconnected and were shut off from the western market by the customs wall of the United States, and so every Canadian who went west was a loss to the country. There is in every country a large number of young men who prefer city life. It was so in Canada. But the provinces had no general policy and did nothing to encourage city industries. The men who could not find city employment in the provinces sought it in the neighboring states, and now there are estimated to be nearly a million Canadians in the United States. Canada, with a population of five millions, has only three cities with over 45,000 inhabitants—Montreal, Toronto and Quebec. Australia has not nearly so large a population as Canada, but it has much larger cities. The reason is that Australia is isolated and forced to depend more upon itself. Americans are fond of referring to Canada as a country deriving all its importance from its proximity to the United States. The fact is that Canada would have been better off to-day if the United States had been on the other side of the globe. If the states had not been so near at hand those city-loving Canadians who crossed the border would have built up cities in their own land, brought about a union of the provinces many years ago and forced the government to encourage manufacturers.

But Canada has little to fear in the future. The Canadian North-West offers greater attractions than any other region open for settlement. Canadian industries are now encouraged and the cities are growing rapidly. Canada's turn is coming. In a few years the available lands in the United States will be taken up and not only will European emigration be diverted to Canada, but thousands of Americans will emigrate to the Canadian North-West. Now, so long as Canada remains independent and shuts out American competition by high protective duties the development of north-western Canada will mean the development of eastern Canada, for the people of the North-West will buy manufactured goods from the east. Were

Canada annexed to the states the manufacturers of eastern Canada would have to compete for the trade of the North-West with manufacturers in both the eastern and western states. They would have little to gain from freedom of access to the United States because most of the western states are already as well developed as the provinces of eastern Canada and in order to divert trade from its present channels and wrest the market from Americans it would be necessary to make extraordinary efforts. Trade forms ruts for itself and it is hard to alter its course. This is well illustrated in newspaper enterprises. A new journal starting in a field already well occupied cannot oust its rivals by equalling them in enterprise. In order to wrest from the older papers their circulation and advertising patronage it must be much more enterprising than they are. So when one city secures the trade of a section of country a new city to compete with it must either have greater natural advantages or greater enterprise. Commercial union or reciprocity with the United States would have been to the advantage of Canada twenty years ago. Had annexation taken place then the country would have adjusted itself to the new relations. The cities would have been built in different places. On the frontier of Ontario at points where trade could be carried on with the states to advantage there is no city of importance. The province of Ontario is almost completely shut off from the states by the great lakes and the St. Lawrence river, the only connecting points being where lakes Huron, St. Clair, and Erie are connected by the St. Clair and Detroit rivers, and lakes Erie and Ontario by the Niagara river. At one of these points where the two countries are connected by a ferry line the great city of Detroit commands the American side of the river. At the other point the river is bridged and Buffalo with its 200,000 people holds the gates. To get into American territory Canadian manufacturers must pass one of these cities. Were the tariff restriction removed Buffalo and Detroit would have free access to the western peninsula of Ontario and would be able to compete for its trade on equal terms with the city of Toronto. No section of the United States would find it more convenient to trade with Ontario cities than with Detroit and Buffalo, but a large part of western Ontario would become tributary to the American cities at the expense of Toronto, Hamilton and London. A small section of American territory would become tributary to Montreal, but that would not compensate the commercial metropolis of Canada for the loss of the North-West trade. The maritime provinces are not so much interested in the North-West trade as Ontario and Quebec, but when several projected short railway lines are completed, having coal and iron in close proximity, they should be able to compete for a portion of that trade. The more trade with the United States is developed the less will be the trade with other countries. The carrying trade betwen Canada and the United States will be done mostly by the railways. That between Canada and other foreign countries must be done by ships. The maritime provinces have special facilities for ship building, and if the confederation is maintained and foreign trade encouraged the ship-building industry must in time give employment to thousands of men.

Undoubtedly annexation would retard the growth of eastern Canada. Now as to its effect upon the North-West. The wonderful progress of the city of Winnipeg has done much toward popularizing the Canadian North-West. Visitors to a new country who have not time to carefully examine its resources take their impressions from the cities. The Canadian Pacific Railway Company recognizes the fact that the progress of Winnipeg will be regarded as an index of the prosperity of the North-West, and accordingly places on all its maps and pamphlets views of Winnipeg in 1870 and 1882. A little to the south of the boundary line, in the state of Minnesota, are three cities very favourably situated for obtaining control of the North-West trade—Minneapolis, St. Paul, and Duluth. Winnipeg has no natural advantages over them, and as St. Paul and Minneapolis are far larger than Winnipeg, they would probably maintain their supremacy if they had free access to the Canadian North-West, but while they remain shut off from it they cannot hope to compete with the Canadian city. The metropolis of the Canadian North-West, whether it be Winnipeg or some other city, controlling the trade of the largest wheat belt in the world will become a second Chicago. The towns west of Winnipeg would not be so much affected at first, but even they would be subject to the competition of the towns to the south. In a few years when the coal and iron industries of the North-West are developed manufactures will be established in these towns and they will be as anxious to shut out competition as Ontario people now are. It may be said that I am discussing this question from a city standpoint, but it is to the interest of the farmers to have a market for their products near at hand, and with prosperous cities they will have a good home market. Farmers living near a large city have better shipping facilities, better newspapers, and greater educational advantages. They are able to preserve their soil by a rotation of crops and are not obliged to pay the cost of freighting their productions to foreign markets.

There has been some talk in Manitoba lately of annexation to the United States. Now, while some of the demands of Manitoba might reasonably be granted, it is a mistake to suppose that it would have what it asks for if it were an American state. Manitoba wants to control its own lands. But the western states that have been carved out of national territory do not control their own lands. The federal government in the United States has control of public lands in all the territories and in states formed out of territories. Manitoba wants the tariff abolished, but as an American state it would have to pay much higher duties although agricultural implements and a few other articles might be somewhat cheaper than they are at present. Manitoba asks for a larger subsidy. As an American state it would have no subsidy, and the expenses of local government which are now paid out of the Dominion treasury would have to be met by direct taxation, which would amount to more than would be saved by the abolition of the duty on agricultural implements. Manitoba wishes to charter railways without fear of disallowance. As an American state it would have that power subject to a decision of the Supreme Court of the United States that no state can pass laws endorsing repudiation or a breach of contract. But the power to charter railways in opposition to the Canadian Pacific would be of no advantage. The railways would be chartered and a few of them would be built and bonussed by the people. After they were built the Canadian Pacific would purchase them and raise freight rates to pay the cost of the useless parallel lines. That is the way the Grand Trunk has done in Ontario, and if Ontario with nearly two million people cannot maintain rival lines of railway, Manitoba is not likely to do it. The Dominion government are well acquainted with the character of the North-West country. They are enthusiastic regarding its future, and are doing all in their power to direct emigration thither. The Dominion Parliament devotes more attention to the affairs of Manitoba and the North-West than to those of all the eastern provinces. In a few years the representatives of the North-West provinces, owing to the rapid increase in population, will have influence enough at Ottawa to carry any reasonable measure. Were Manitoba an American state matters now conducted by the Ottawa government would be looked after by the government at Washington, which would know less about the country and would have comparatively little interest in its development. Manitoba's influence in the United States Congress would be insignificant and if its representatives talked secession they would be laughed at. Indeed, it is not likely that Manitoba would have any higher status than a territory for some time to come. Dakota has a larger population than Manitoba and it for years petitioned in vain for the rights of a state, while Manitoba was long ago admitted as a province of the Dominion, and Saskatchewan, Assinaboia, Alberta and Athabaska will become provinces before they are as populous as Dakota. The North-west territories of Canada will soon surpass Manitoba in population and if Manitoba cities would control the trade of that great country they must uphold the Dominion of Canada and shut out American competition. Already the people of Manitoba complain that immigrants are passing by their fertile lands and staking claims farther west. Manitoba will need the tariff to hold the trade of the more western provinces and territories just as Ontario needs the tariff to retain the trade of Manitoba. The future of Manitoba depends very largely upon the prosperity of the Canadian Pacific Railway. That railway runs east and west, connecting the various provinces of the Dominion. If the provinces trade with the adjoining states instead of with one another traffic will go north and south instead of east and west and the Canadian Pacific railway will hardly pay running expenses.

Canada has the finest fisheries in the world. The people of the United States have no fisheries of importance, and as they seem anxious to give up the privilege of fishing in Canadian waters there will be additional work for Canadian fishermen in supplying the American market. Of course, in abrogating the treaty the Americans will probably impose a duty on fish which now enter the United States free, but since they cannot supply their own market, even with their present privileges, they will not be able to do so when they are shut out of Canadian waters, and although the imposition of a duty on fish would raise the price in the United States it would not shut out Canadian fish unless the increase in price greatly reduced the consumption. It is possible that the discussion of the fishery question may lead to the negotiation of a reciprocity treaty with the United States. Now, while full reciprocity with the United States would be most injurious to Canada reciprocity in natural productions would probably be beneficial, but Canadian statesmen should be careful not to grant too much. The duties on the manufactured products of the United States should in no case be removed or reduced.

Many Canadian freetraders would be quite willing to maintain the protective tariff against

England, provided an American zollverein could be established. Canada has less to fear from British manufacturers than from Americans. An imperial zollverein would at least have the effect of building up two or three great importing cities, while with an American zollverein American manufacturers holding the gates of commerce, as I have shown, would deal directly with retail dealers. But the true policy for Canada is neither an imperial zollverein nor an American zollverein. It is a colonial zollverein. As I pointed out in the Century magazine some time ago a protective tariff should be a discriminating tariff so arranged as to shut off the competition of strong manufacturing nations while encouraging trade with countries likely to afford a market for manufactured products. The right of the self-governing colonies to arrange a system of differential duties between each other has already been acknowledged by Great Britain. By arranging for free trade with the Australian colonies, South Africa and the West Indies Canada would secure greater advantages than by an American zollverein. As the colonies became entirely independent the system could be extended to include Brazil and other South

American countries. In this way could be secured all the advantages of free trade with none of its disadvantages. The competition of strong manufacturing nations would be shut off while Canadian manufacturers would have a greatly extended field. Canada was intended by nature to be a great shipping country. It has better harbors on both the Atlantic and Pacific coasts than the United States with every facility for ship building, and its inter-oceanic railway is the shortest across the continent, so that a great part of the trade between Asia and Europe must go over it to be shipped again from Canadian ports on Canadian vessels.

When a country reaches a certain stage of progress, when its people are unquestionably able to compete successfully with all other nations absolute free trade may best advance its interests. Britain reached that position about fifty years ago. The United States will reach it before many years go by. It will be a long time before Canada attains to that position. When the British adopted free trade they had no need of protection. The danger was that other countries would adopt high protective tariffs that would shut out British goods. The

British had two objects in view in adopting free trade. The one was to secure cheap food for their artisans. The other was to set an example that all other countries would imitate. Had the whole world adopted free trade when Britain did the British might always have retained their supremacy as a manufacturing people. But other countries were not so ready to imitate as was expected. One of the circulars issued by members of the Cobden Club said : "It is our creed that if America will put down her monopolizing manufacturers when our election time comes we will lay Manchester and Sheffield alongside of Indiana and Illinois, the finest states of the union. This artisan and this mechanic will manufacture for them and they will grow food for us." But the Americans looked at the question from a different standpoint. They thought it would be better to do their own manufacturing and so they established a system of protection.

Canada is not in the position that England was in 1842 as regards the markets of the world, but there are many countries with which Canada could profitably negotiate free trade treaties. Canadians should discriminate. They should protect themselves against the encroachments of great manufacturing nations and make friendly overtures to countries where manufacturing industries are not well developed. If it were possible to arrange a zollverein with all young countries Canadians would have access to the most profitable markets in the world, while all the great manufacturing nations would be cut off from them. It may be impossible to accomplish that, but an approach may be made to it. It is now the policy of the Dominion government to encourage trade with countries like Brazil and the West Indies. That policy should be prosecuted with renewed vigor. Every effort should be made to arrange a zollverein with such countries, and where that cannot be done reciprocity treaties should be negotiated.

There are some densely populated countries with which reciprocity treaties might be negotiated to advantage, notably China and Japan. China is the most important foreign consumer of United States cottons and Canadian cotton manufacturers might do a large business in that country.

It is true that without the extension of colonial privileges the colonies could not form a zollverein that would include foreign countries like Brazil and exclude England. At present England would probably insist on being placed on equal terms with other countries. But the steps of the colonies toward independence have been continuous. The establishment of the Canadian protective tariff was the last step. It was not favorably regarded by the English, but they did not object, and if a further step is taken it is not likely to cause much trouble. In 1877 Phillips Thompson, of Toronto, one of the ablest of Canadian journalists, wrote from Boston, where he was then temporarily residing, to the Right Hon. William Ewart Gladstone, of England, as follows :—

SIR,—The question of reciprocal free trade between the United States and Canada excites some interest here. In connection with the discussion the question has been raised as to whether, in the event of negotiations being entered into with the object of a Reciprocity Treaty, England would insist that Canada should admit English manufactures on the same terms as she might agree to extend to American goods of the same class. In other words, would the Canadians be permitted, under treaty, to give advantages to Americans which were withheld from their British fellow subjects. The question, though apparently a side issue of not much importance from an American standpoint, has really a great deal to do with deciding the practicability of a comprehensive treaty. Pardon, therefore, the liberty I take in asking what is the traditional policy in relation to the matter ? and whether the present government have made any decisive statement as to their course in such an event ? for, if I mistake not, the question did come up for consideration a few years ago, when a treaty was under discussion. The fact that business men and others interested wish to obtain some definite information on a point little understood in this country before the matter comes up during the approaching session of Congress, must be my apology for troubling you.

Very respectfully,
PHILLIPS THOMPSON.

Mr. Gladstone replied as follows :—

ENNISKERRY, October 30th.
Phillips Thompson, Esq., Boston,
Sir,—The question you put is one of much difficulty, and I am unable to give you an answer which could or ought to guide you or others. No other country except this would, however, I think, regard it as an open one, and in this country I think the decision would depend mainly on the views and leanings of the Colonial Minister and the government of the day.

Your very faithful, etc.,
W. E. GLADSTONE.

Mr. Gladstone's letter was rather non-committal, but one would scarcely think after reading it that differentiation against England would lead to bloodshed, and yet in 1874 the British government announced that no treaty would be sanctioned which should place English exporters at a disadvantage as compared with Americans. But fortunately there need be no occasion for trouble between Canada and England on that account. Full reciprocity with the United States would be a great in-

jury to Canada, and Canadians are not likely
to fight for it. Natural productions might be
admitted free and the same privileges might be
extended to England for Canada is now in a
position to compete with the world in natural
productions. But if there is any doubt in the
minds of British statesmen regarding the advisability of opposing the commercial union of
Canada and the United States they surely
would not make very much trouble on account
of a zollverein which would include a young
country like Brazil and exclude the United
States as well as England.

Without any extension of their present
powers the self-governing colonies can arrange
a colonial zollverein excluding Britain and all
other countries. That was conceded by the British government when the Dominion government
insisted upon the right of the colonies to arrange
a system of differential duties with one another.
The British colonies in Australia and South
Africa are discussing confederation schemes,
and now is the time to press upon their attention the advantages that all would derive from
a colonial zollverein. A clause of the Canadian
Customs Act provides that whenever the
Americans are willing to reciprocate natural

productions will be admitted free. In order to induce Australia, South Africa and other countries to form a zollverein with Canada it might be necessary to strike out that clause and engage to maintain a high protective tariff against all imports from the United States because the natural products of some of the states to the south would come into competition with those of the warmer colonies.

There is a way in which England might be induced to look favorably upon a colonial zollverein. Canada now imposes the same duties on British manufactures as on American manufactures. The Australian colonies will soon be confederated and they may at any time adopt a protective system similar to that of Canada. If the present system is continued Britain will gradually be shut out from all her colonies. But the colonies joining the zollverein might agree to differentiate in favor of Britain. A high tariff could be maintained against Britain for purposes of revenue and protection, but still higher duties would be imposed upon goods from the United States and other foreign countries. This system would give the British a slight advantage over all other nations not within the zollverein, whi'e it would not permit them to crush out colonial manufacturers. Canadians have a most friendly feeling toward the Americans and would dislike to discriminate in favor of England but it might be easier to induce the other colonies to join the zollverein if England put no obstacles in the way.

With a colonial zollverein in force British Columbia would become one of the most important of Canadian provinces. There would be built upon its coast at the terminus of the Canadian Pacific railway a city that would rival San Francisco. The exhaustless coal mines, the great forests, the wonderful fisheries of the province would all be utilized, and, possessing a larger domain than Ontario, it might dispute with it for the title of the premier province. Let us keep our own markets by maintaining a high protective tariff against the United States, England and other great manufacturing countries and make new markets by negotiating free trade treaties with young countries all over the world.

Canada has nothing to gain commercially by annexation to the United States, and apart from commercial considerations all the provinces are interested in the maintenance of the confederation. The governmental institutions of the United States were deliberately created one hundred years ago. Those of Canada are being gradually evolved by the popular will. There still remain in the Canadian system many rudimentary formalities. They served a purpose once : they are useless now and will be lopped off in a few years. The present constitution has always been regarded as temporary and experimental. The framers of the American constitution had little to go by in the way of experience. When the representatives of the Canadian people meet to declare the country independent and frame a new constitution they will be guided not only by their own experiments but by the experience of the Americans, and with the opportunities they have enjoyed of noting the operation of the American constitution and comparing it with others they should, in the light of their own experience, be able to produce a constitution superior to any in existence. Even now the Canadian system has certain advantages over that of the United States. There can be no doubt in the minds of Canadians that their judical system is superior to that of the republic, and that is, perhaps, the most important department of the government.

Canadians so far as regards their customs and institutions can hardly be called an original people. They are rather imitative. In some respects they copy the English and French; in others they imitate the Americans. But there is one institution which is peculiar to Canada, and Canadians have no reason to be proud of it. There is nothing exactly like the Canadian Senate anywhere else in the world. It is probably the result of an attempt to copy both the British House of Lords and the United States Senate. The House of Lords and the United States Senate are both representative bodies and both are logical outcomes of the governmental systems of which they form a part. The British people are divided into two classes, the aristocrats and the plebians. The one is represented by the House of Lords, the other by the House of Commons. The United States is a federation of sovereign states. The House of Congress represents the various sections of the republic at large. The Senate represents the states as individuals. Upper houses are maintained rather as a check upon lower houses than with a view to the initiation of legislation. Were it not for the restraining influence of the House of Lords the privileges of the aristocratic classes of Britain would soon be abolished and the two sections of the British people would gradually be merged into one. If the American Senate were abolished the United States would become a consolidation like the Dominion of Canada instead of a federal union of sovereign states. To abolish the British House of Lords or the Senate of the United States would be to interfere with the fundamental principles of government in those countries. The abolition of the Dominion Senate would in no way affect the Canadian system of government. It represents no section and no interest. Canada is a democracy and there is no aristocracy to be preserved. It is a consolidation rather than a federation and there are no sovereign states to be represented. There is no reason for the existence of the Canadian Senate; it will certainly be abolished in a few years; and now is the time to consider what shall take its place or whether it is necessary to have more than one house of Parliament. The uselessness of the Senate as at present constituted is apparent to everybody, but there is difference of opinion

as to what should succeed it. Many believe
the senate should be elected by the provincial
legislatures just as the United States Senate is
elected by the state legislatures. The adoption of that system would mean a complete
change in the form of government. Canada
would cease to be a consolidated Dominion
and become a federation of sovereign states.
Would it be a change for the better ? I think
not. The American system is not democratic.
The name " Democratic " is as inapplicable to
the American party which it designates as the
name " Reform " is to the Grit party of Canada.
The Democratic party of the United States
has always contended for the maintenance of
state rights and yet the United States can
never be a democracy so long as the states remain sovereign and retain their present rights.
The American system is not democratic because each state is regarded as an individual.
The little state of Rhode Island with its small
population has the same representation in the
United States Senate as the great state of New
York. Texas is large enough and fertile
enough to support thirty million people. It
will, no doubt, have that many inhabitants
some day. Nevada is nothing but a worked

out mining region. It has no agricultural resources and the population is decreasing instead of increasing. The population is so
small that it only has one representative in the
United States House of Congress and yet it
has the same number of representatives in the
United States Senate as the great state of
Texas. The number of senators is fixed at two
for each state independent and irrespective of
the size of the state or the number of its inhabitants. Should Canada adopt the American
system the few thousand people living in Prince
Edward Island would have as much power in
the decision of many important questions as
the millions of people living in Ontario. The
combined populations of Prince Edward Island
and British Columbia would scarcely outnumber the inhabitants of three or four counties
of Ontario, but those provinces could out-vote
Ontario in the Senate. It would be better to
have no Senate at all or even to continue the
present absurdity than to adopt the undemocratic system of the United States. Canada
has now the most democratic form of government of any country in the world. Any changes
made should be in the direction of making it
more democratic rather than less so.

No question has excited more interest in Canada of late years than that of the exercise of the veto power. An examination of the veto systems of Canada and the United States suggests an idea that may help to solve the Senate question. Nominally the Governor-General of Canada has the right to veto the legislation of the Dominion Parliament, but that right has been declared obsolete. The lieutenant-governors of the provinces also have nominal veto powers which are never exercised. But the right of the governor-general-in-council to disallow measures passed by the provincial legislatures is freely exercised. The giving of nominal veto powers to the governor-general and the provincial governors was an unreasoning imitation of the British system. So far as regards Great Britain, Canada and Australia the British empire is an imperial federation with parliaments distinct and independent, the crown being the only bond of union. The queen through the governor-general has the same relation to the Canadian parliament that she has to the British parliament, but her power is only nominal. As in England the queen is guided entirely by the advice of her cabinet, so in Canada the governor-general, her representative, is guided entirely by the advice of his cabinet, and this is why the governor-general can without any instructions from either the queen or Parliament of England fully represent the queen in Canada. Just as the governor-general represents the queen in Dominion matters so the lieutenant-governors represent the governor-general in provincial matters and the same imaginary powers are given to them for the sake of form.

But the disallowance of provincial legislation by the Dominion government is a different matter. That is not a rudimentary remnant of an obsolete system. It is the outcome of the deliberate consideration of the representatives of the Canadian people. The leading men of both political parties agreed that it was necessary to the maintenance of the Dominion. It serves two purposes, preventing sectional legislation that would prove injurious to the Dominion at large and providing for the representation of minorities, for although the Dominion can in no way dictate legislation for the provinces it can refuse to sanction a provincial measure, and in the event of unjust legislation the minority can appeal to it. For instance, in Quebec province the English

speaking people form a minority of the population and have very few representatives in the
Quebec legislature. That legislature might
pass laws doing decided injustice to the
English speaking people, but the minority
could appeal to the Dominion government and
the laws would be vetoed. In Ontario on the
other hand, the French Canadians are in the
minority. There are many thousands of them
in the province and they are increasing very
rapidly but they have no influence in the
Ontario legislature as yet. The Ontario
legislature might sometime pass laws bearing
unjustly on the French Canadians. The minority would appeal to the Dominion government which would disallow the bills. Edward
Blake has often theorized regarding the advantages of minority representation. To be
consistent he should boldly support disallowance. The veto power in Canada like the
Senate of the United States is a part of a
system. Its abolition would completely alter
the system.

The veto power as exercised in the United
States is quite different. It is intended to
counteract the evils attending sectional representation. The workings of the system are

well illustrated in the government of cities.
Take the city of Buffalo for example. The city
council is composed of representatives from
the various wards. One alderman wishes to
secure a necessary improvement in his ward.
His re-election depends upon his success in
obtaining a grant for that purpose. Other
aldermen oppose him. They wish to secure
expenditures in their wards which he considers
extravagant and fraudulent. But he cannot
carry his point without their support. They
will not support him unless he reciprocates,
and the result is a general grab. Men disposed to be honest and economical themselves
are obliged to support extravagant if not
dishonest measures in order to secure necessary
improvements in their sections. The aldermen
represent the wards, but the mayor represents
the city at large. He vetoes the obnoxious
measures. Governor Cleveland gained such
popularity by his vetoes while mayor of Buffalo
that he was carried to the gubernatorial chair
on a great popular wave. His election was
due to other causes, perhaps, but he undoubtedly owed his nomination to his record
as a veto mayor. Just as the wards of a city
are represented by aldermen so the various

sections of the state are represented by assemblymen. They, like aldermen, would often pass bad bills and for the same reason, but while the assemblymen are elected by the various districts the governor is elected by the state at large and holds the assemblymen in check with his vetoes. So with the United States Congress and the president. The House of Congress represents the various districts of the country ; the Senate represents the states ; the president represents the country at large. Certain congressmen living near the Mississippi river represent men who own large tracts of land made valueless by Mississippi floods. If the mighty river can be kept within its bounds these lands will become very valuable. These congressmen ask for a large grant of money for that purpose. Other congressmen oppose them until all agree to make a general raid on the treasury and the River and Harbor bill is originated. Each congressman secures a grant for his district and vast sums of money are granted for the improvement of dried up creeks that can never be made navigable. The bill is the result of sectional representation and the president who represents the people at large, vetoes it, but a two-thirds majority in both houses enables the sections to carry their point and override the veto.

The evils of sectional representation are apparent in Canada as well as in the United States. The Canadian Pacific Railway Com. pany contracted with the government to complete the line from Montreal to the Pacific Ocean by the year 1891. The work was carried on with marvellous rapidity for a few years and the company announced to the public that they would have the road completed in 1886 instead of 1891. But owing to the opposition of the Grand Trunk and Northern Pacific railways and the misrepresentations of certain Canadian newspapers they were unable to borrow money in Europe to finish the work and accordingly asked the Dominion government for a loan of nearly thirty million dollars, stating that unless that amount was raised the work of construction would be stopped for a time. In stopping work they would not violate their contract. They were not obliged to complete the road before 1891 and they had already constructed the greater part of it. But stoppage of work on the great Canadian highway would have caused a panic. The stock of the company, already depressed, would have become almost worthless ; thousands of men would have been thrown out of employment ; the credit of Canada in Europe would have been destroyed and the very existence of the Dominion would have been imperiled. The proposal of the company just amounted to this. They were unable at that time to borrow money in Europe at any price. The government coul1 borrow money at four per cent. The railway offered the government five per cent. for a loan or in other words asked the government to act as agent for it in the European market on consideration cf a commission of one per cent. It would cost the country nothing ; it would make no difference to the taxpayer and the great national railway would be completed in five years before the expiration of the time allowed by the contract. It was provided in the agreement submitted to Parliament that in case of failure to pay the interest or the principal the whole line of railway with its rolling stock should at once become government property and every employe of the company a government employe. The security was good. There was no risk. The arrangement would not increase taxation by one cent. It would insure the speedy construction of the railway and avert a panic. But when Parliament was asked to sanction the agreement between the company and the government the representatives from Quebec demanded that a large sum be expended in Quebec as the price of their vote. Most of the Reform members from Ontario supported the Bleus of Quebec in their opposition to the loan and the result was that in order to secure the passage of the resolutions the government was obliged to yield to the demand of the Quebec representatives. Now, I do not propose to discuss in this connection the justice of Quebec's claims. I am disposed to think that the opening up of the province by railways will be of advantage to the whole Dominion just as the building of the Canadian Pacific railway through North-West Ontario and the Canadian North-West will open up new markets and make the whole country more prosperous. But however that may be the demand of the Quebec representatives at that time when the interests of the whole Dominion were jeopardised was due to the same sectional feeling that gave birth to the River and Harbor bill in the United States.

No modification of the representative

system of government could entirely abolish this evil, but it might be possible to check it somewhat. The principle of the veto as exercised in the United States is a good one, and if the Canadian and American veto systems were combined in a certain way, the result would be a body of senators fully in accord with the Canadian system of government. The Canadian House of Commons represents the various sections of the Dominion. Suppose the Senate were elected by the cumulative vote of the Dominion at large. The members of the lower house would look after the interests of the sections which they represented and the upper house would see that the interests of the Dominion were not sacrificed to satisfy sectional greed or jealousy. The Senate need not be a large body. A small number of eminent men elected by the whole Canadian people would exercise a great influence for good. The Senate would be a vetoing body. The vetoing powers now possessed by the Dominion ministry could be transferred to it and it would of course have power to veto the measures of the House of Parliament. The election of senators by the Dominion at large would insure a thorough study of their characters by the

Canadian people. The men elected to the Senate would be known throughout the country. They would be described in all the newspapers. The story of their lives would become common property. Their pictures would be in every house. The senators like the members of Parliament would be elected at stated periods and being responsible to the people would be careful not to excite popular indignation by abusing their powers, while they would carefully watch the legislation of Parliament and the legislatures lest their enactments prove injurious to the Dominion. Such a senate would not be a perfect body. It is impossible to secure perfect government so long as men are imperfect, but it would be superior to both the United States Senate and the Canadian Senate as now constituted. Not only is the American system undemocratic because it gives a state with a population of one hundred thousand the same representation in the Senate as a state with five million inhabitants, but the mode of election affords great opportunities for corruption. If you wish to persuade a body of men to do a wrong thing you must talk to each one alone: advise a great crowd of men to commit an act of injustice or endorse a mean action and they will greet you with a storm of hisses. Whisper the same thing in the ear of each one and it will be received by many of them in quite a different way. A corrupt man will find it easier to obtain the support of a legislature than to get the votes of a whole people. The people as a unit are almost incorruptible. As individuals they are very easily corrupted. The position of senator under the system proposed would be a most honorable one. The ablest and noblest men in the land would aspire to it. The thought that he might some day be a senator would be a great incentive to many a boy and the whole people would take a greater interest in the deliberations of the Senate than in those of any other department of the government.

The advisability of giving the Dominion Senate the power to veto provincial legislation may be questioned. There are some reasons why that power should be abolished altogether. As has already been said it provides for the representation of minorities and prevents sectional legislation injurious to the Dominion at large. But it has a tendency to antagonize Dominion and provincial authorities. What-

ever may be said on the question of minority
representation it is quite certain that local
legislatures should not be permitted to pass
laws endangering the welfare of the whole
Canadian people and if the power of the
Dominion to veto local legislation is abolished
all questions of national concern must be
brought within the jurisdiction of the Dominion
Parliament and the powers of the local legislatures must be so restricted that it will be impossible for them to legislate on matters
affecting the whole Dominion. The right to
charter railways must be withdrawn and all
laws affecting the commerce of the country
must be enacted by the Dominion Parliament.

The great danger of Canada is provincialism. A strong central government is more
necessary in Canada than in the United States
because there are more outside influences at
work. When the great republic was in its in-
fancy there was no other power on the
continent. Canada for many years to come
will have reason to fear the country to the
south ; not because the United States is
likely to wage war with Canada but because
anything that draws a province into closer

union with the states adjoining it weakens the
bonds of union between the provinces. Indeed,
nothing would tend so much to bind the
provinces together and weld the various
nationalities into one as a war in defence of the
Dominion that would fire popular enthusiasm,
kindle national pride, and bring the people
together. It was such a war as that which
laid the foundation of American nationalism.
But it is not likely that Canada will ever have
a war, and the provinces instead of being
forced together by outside pressure must be
cemented by common laws and great national
measures. The Canadian system recognizes
no provincial boundaries except for purposes
of local government. If the boundaries of the
provinces were wiped out altogether it would
make no difference in the method of selecting
the general government. In this respect the
Canadian system is radically different from
that of the United States. But, nevertheless,
provincial lines are too much considered in
the discussion of national questions and the
vetoing of provincial legislation, by antago-
nizing Dominion and provincial authorities,
helps to perpetuate provincial jealousy. The
men who revise the constitution when Canada

becomes independent may decide to restrict the powers of the provincial legislatures and withdraw the veto power from the Dominion authorities, thus making the provincial legislatures supreme in regard to the matters with which they have to deal, while giving the Dominion Parliament jurisdiction in all matters that concern the people generally. If so, the Dominion Senate under the system proposed would have nothing to do with provincial matters. It would discuss only national questions.

In the *Popular Science Monthly* for February, 1883, Prof. E. W. Gilliam showed that in 1960, during the lifetime of many people now living, there will be ninety-six million blacks in the southern states and that long before that they will far outnumber the whites. In the *North American Review* for July, 1884, Charles A. Gardiner says :—

If a straight line should be drawn from the northern border of Delaware to the north-eastern corner of Kansas, and one from that point south to the Gulf of Mexico, nineteen-twentieths of the negro race in America would be found east and south of these lines. But taking the Atlantic and Gulf states, North Carolina, South Carolina, Georgia, Florida, Alabama, Mississippi and Louisiana, we have a compact territory, uniform in climate and resources, and inhabited by two-thirds of all the negroes in the United States. The actual occupancy of the soil and the providential adaptation of the race to its physical surroundings suggest that this territory will be the future home of the negro race.   The census of 1880 discloses the fact that the native white population had increased twenty per cent. in the past ten years, and that the negro population had increased thirty-five per cent. in the same time.   Increasing two per cent. annually whites double in every thirty-five years, while negroes, increasing three and a half per cent. annually will double in every twenty years.   In the year 1882-83, 400,000 foreigners landed in the United States ; of this number only 736 settled in the seven states named above.   With due allowance for foreign and northern immigration it still seems a reasonable conjecture that, adopting the ratios established, within sixty years negroes will be in the majority in all the south, and that one hundred years from to-day they will be doub'e the number of whites in every southern state.   The following table indicates the present and estimated future population of the Atlantic and Gulf states :

WHITES.		NEGROES.	
1880.....	3,814,395	1880..........	3,721,481
1915..........	7,600,000	1900..........	7,400,000
1950..........	15,200,000	1920..........	14,800,000
1985..........	30,400,000	1940..........	29,600,000
		1960..........	59,200,000
		1980..........	118,400,000

In discussing this question Canon Rawlinson and other miscegenists have made a common initial blunder. They have assumed that the 6,500,000 negroes would gradually disperse throughout the United States and would be absorbed by the 43,000,000 whites.   Present indications are against this assumption.   The negro will doubtless remain in the seven states designated.   Southern estimates show that a legitimate amalgamation is slowly beginning between the races ; this will continue.   The negro is acquiring land, becoming educated, gradually asserting and maintaining his legal and political rights and approaching more and more to the social level of the whites.   Fifty years from now in the aggregate of numbers and of wealth, the negro outside of the sea-port cities will be the superior, the Caucasian the inferior race. The wealthy and enterprising whites will gradually migrate to the border states or to the seaboard cities, while those who have so far degenerated from their race pride and race spirit as to prefer such supremacy to emigration will gradually be absorbed and controlled by the negro. In no case does the mixed people show the mental vigor of the Caucasian parent stock, and in most instances the mental and moral condition of the half castes is lower even than that of the inferior parent stock.

It will be observed that Prof. E. W. Gilliam's estimate of the negro population in 1960 is larger than that of Mr. Gardiner. This is because the former includes a larger number of states in his estimate. Outside of the seven states mentioned there is a large negro population in the South and even in the North, according to the New York *Sun*, they hold the balance of power in New York, Pennsylvania, Ohio, Indiana and Connecticut. Their influence in these states, however, would always be insignificant were it not for the natural inclination to side with the blacks of the South in case of a race struggle of any sort. There are already nearly seven million negroes in the United States, and whether they concentrate in the South or not they must in a few years exert an important influence on the government of a country where manhood suffrage prevails.

Canadians have no desire to be governed either by negroes or the class of white politicians most likely to control negro votes, nor do they wish to have any part in the disputes that must arise between the two races, perhaps ending in a bloody war.

Much has been said of the liberty of the United States. There is no more liberty in the states than in the provinces ; but there is more license. License is a diseased form of liberty. Government cannot be successfully based upon the idea that every man has a right to do as he pleases. Whenever the people of the United States have acted as a unit, losing sight of sectional or individual interests, their policy has been a grand success. When they have gone to the other extreme they have made a failure. This is well illustrated in the evils resulting from the laxity of marriage and divorce laws. The divorce statistics of the United States are startling, and thousands of Canadians would oppose annexation on this account if there were no other objection. In some cases divorces conduce to happiness, but laws cannot be made to suit exceptional cases. They must be framed with a view to the welfare of the people at large, and undoubtedly it is better to have no divorce at all than to permit it on flimsy pretexts. There is little to be gained by divorce in any case. There is the same chance that a mistake will be made in the second marriage as in the first. When people understand that marriages are made for better or for worse they are likely to be careful whom they marry and make the best of it when disappointed in their expectations. It is not very pleasant for a pure minded woman to be tied for life to a drunken husband, but then the chances are that if divorced she would marry another drunkard. If she could not distinguish between the good and the bad in selecting her first husband she would probably do no better in making a second choice. Moreover a divorced woman has not so many opportunities to make the acquaintance of good men as when she lived at home before her first marriage. The best men do not, as a rule, care to marry divorced women. If the first marriage was unhappy the second marriage is almost certain to be more so. It is impossible to make laws that will provide for everybody and supply people with common sense. If home happiness is commonly destroyed by liquor drinking the way to remedy the evil is not to break up the home by divorce but to prohibit the manufacture of liquor.

Canadians believe in stringent marriage and divorce laws. They believe that on account of constant migration between the provinces the divorce laws should be the same throughout the Dominion. Divorces are now almost unknown in Canada. According to figures in the *North American Review* in St. Louis in 1879 the number of divorces was one to every 700 inhabitants. In San Francisco in 1880 the number of divorces was one to every 702 inhabitants, while in Connecticut the ratio of divorces to population was about one in 1906, and in Massachusetts in 1878 it was about one to 2971. In Wayne county, Mich., containing 200,000 inhabitants there was a ratio of one divorce to 796 of the population, and in Kent county in 1881 there were 921 marriages and 202 divorce suits in a population of 75,000. Connecticut has during the last 21 years had an annual average of about one divorce to 11 marriages; Vermont for 19 years has had one divorce to 17 marriages; Massachusetts for 19 years has had one divorce to 35 marriages.

In a recent article in the *Contemporary Re-*

view Mr. Goldwin Smith endeavored to prove
that Canada is physically divided in such a
way that national unity. is impossible. He
says: " Canada proper, besides being divided
internally between the British colony and New
France, is separated from Manitoba and the
prairie region of the North-West by the great
fresh water sea, called Lake Superior, while it
is united to the state of New York and to
Pennsylvania from which it draws its coal."
By Canada proper Mr. Smith means Ontario
and Quebec. As I have stated Ontario is not
very closely connected with the states and a
glance at the map of North America will con-
vince anyone that Lake Superior does not
sever the province of Ontario from the Canadian North-West. Lake Superior separates
the province of Ontario from the states of
Michigan, Wisconsin and Minnesota, but the
only boundary between Ontario and Manitoba
is an artificial one—so artificial that there was
for years a dispute as to where it lay, one party
claiming that the town of Rat Portage was
within the province of Ontario, and the other
that it was within the boundaries of Manitoba.
Nor is it true that the maritime provinces
are separated from Canada proper by an

irreclaimable wilderness. Much of the country is unsettled, it is true, but there are some very valuable lands in that section and in time they will be all occupied. It is not so well adapted to the production of wheat as some other sections but it is a fine grazing country and the minerals are very valuable. British Columbia is separated from the North-West by the Rocky Mountains, but so is California separated from the western states by the Rockies. Mr. Smith does not predict the disruption of the United States on that account.

What Mr. Smith says about Quebec province, or New France, as he calls it, is partly true. The old French language and the old French customs still largely prevail there, but it is not true that there is any thought of reviving the connection with France. The French-Canadian and the modern Frenchman are altogether unlike in character and disposition. The climate of Canada has wrought a great change in the character of the race and the sturdy, pious, industrious habitant of Quebec is disposed to regard the fickle and infidel Frenchman with dislike. French immigrants say that they are boycotted by the habitants. The French language is still generally spoken

but English is the language of commerce
and in the centers of commerce the majority
are familiar with both languages. The French-
Canadians are very patriotic. They have
lived in Canada so long that they seem almost
to have sprung from the soil itself. But they
cannot be expected to have much British sentiment. They are proud of the vast Dominion,
and when it becomes independent the French
language will gradually become obsolete as the
national sentiment grows. If the French-
Canadians were confined to Quebec province there would be some reason in Mr.
Smith's contention that they will bring about
a disruption of the confederation ; but there
are many thousands of them in Ontario, the
maritime provinces and Manitoba. An effort
is now being made to induce French-Canadians
who have emigrated to the states to return to
Canada and take up land in the North-West.
A large number have already done so and it is
expected that thousands will follow them next
year. French - Canadians seldom become
American citizens. They always look with
longing eyes on Canada, and if they are suc-
cessful in making money they usually return to
Canada to spend it. Fifty years from now

there will be more French-Canadians in Ontario and the North-West than in Quebec province. The west was first explored by the French-Canadians. They gave their names to many of the rivers and islands and they will play an important part in the future of Canada. They have been much misrepresented and much abused in certain quarters and they certainly are very unprogressive in many respects, but if conclusions can be drawn from the history of other northern nations there will some day come a great waking up, and then the progress of the Canadian people will astonish the world.

Mr. Smith refers to United Empire Loyalists and says that even among them the anti-American sentiment can hardly be said to be intense. The descendants of United Empire loyalists are really more like the Americans than any other class of the Canadian people. Many families can look back upon two hundred years of life in America and they feel more akin to the Americans than to the English. Mr. Smith's mistake is in supposing that anti-American sentiment is essential to the growth of Canadian sentiment. The national sentiment is probably stronger among descendants of United

Empire Loyalists than among any other class of the people. While a few of them still retain the old British sentiment that inspired their ancestors the majority care nothing now about the unity of the empire, but they care a great deal about the unity of Canada.

Mr. Smith thinks the people apart from the politicians are not opposed to annexation. The sentiment of the people is generally voiced, to some extent, by the newspapers. Canada is a big country and there are many newspapers, but I do not know of one daily that openly advocates annexation. But Mr. Smith says the press is in the hands of the party politicians. Well, there are a number of independent papers that have no connection with either party. They do not favor annexation. In Toronto there are three independent dailies— The *News*, *World* and *Telegram*. All of them advocate Canadian independence; none of them advocates annexation. The *News*, which, under the able management of Mr. E. E. Sheppard, has secured an immense circulation, well illustrates the mistake Mr. Smith makes in supposing that an anti-American sentiment is essential to Canadian nationalism. The *News* urges the adoption of the American system of government, praises American customs an 1 in every way endeavors to inculcate American ideas ; but it opposes annexation, believing complete independence more desirable. The *World* is strongly national, opposing every sort of connection, political or commercial, with the United States and endeavoring to encourage Canadian sentiment. The *Telegram* is non-committal. In Montreal there are two independent English dailies, the *Star* and the *Witness* : neither favors annexation. The *Star*, which has the largest circulation of any paper published in Quebec province favors Canadian independence. The *Witness* favors a legislative union of the provinces. In Winnipeg there is one independent daily, the *Sun*. It advocates Canadian independence and opposes annexation. There are a few papers which incline to favor annexation although they do not openly advocate it. The St. Catharines *News*, a Reform newspaper does, not exactly advocate annexation but it makes a very near approach to it. The Bobcaygeon *Independent*, an independent Reform weekly which has attracted some notice by its able editorials, thinks annexation is inevitable although it declares its dislike for American institutions. Several Reform papers in Nova Scotia are advocating secession from the Dominion. They do not declare in favor of annexation, but secession would, of course, result in annexation.

Mr. Goldwin Smith since he came to Canada has endeavored at one time in the *Nation*, again in the *Bystander*, and now in the *Week* by pessimistic predictions regarding the future of the Dominion to arouse an annexation sentiment. He is held in high esteem by men of all parties and is regarded as the most polished writer in Canada, and yet he has failed to persuade a single politician or newspaper to openly advocate annexation. There is no better illustration of the fact that the Canadian people do not believe in annexation. But an opportunity was afforded a Toronto audience not long ago to express an opinion in this regard. Sir Richard Cartwright, one of the leaders of the Reform party and Minister of Finance during the Mackenzie administration, addressed a large audience in the Grand Opera House at Toronto on the 20th of May. After comparing the cost of government in the two countries, overlooking, as Mr. Smith has done, the whole cost of state government, he said there was undoubtedly in the minds of Canadians a feeling of great unrest ; a feeling that the present position of Canada and the present form of government could not long continue : there must be a change. What that change should be was a question for debate. It might be annexation. To this proposition the audience made no response, although he waited for an expression of opinion. There was quietness in the house save for a few hisses. Then he proceeded to say that he did not believe in annexation and the audience loudly applauded. But there might be independence without annexation. This suggestion was received with wild applause—clapping of hands, stamping of feet and cheering. He had often thought that imperial federation would be a grand scheme. The audience did not seem to think so for it failed to respond to the suggestion, but when he said he had only reference to a defensive alliance between all English-speaking nations there was some applause.

Mr. Smith says the churches entirely disregard the boundary line. There is no connection between the churches of Canada and the United States excepting that of Christian sympathy which exists between the churches of all countries. The Roman Catholic church being governed from Rome cannot be a distinctively Canadian church, but the tendency of all Protestant bodies is toward Canadianism. The most important Protestant churches in Canada are the Presbyterians and Methodists. All the Presbyterians of Canada united some time ago, forming a distinctively Canadian church, and a union of all the Methodist denominations in the Canadian provinces has just been consummated. Leading Presbyterians and Methodists have expressed the opinion that these amalgamations are but steps to the union of the Presbyterians and Methodists in one great Canadian Protestant church. In the United States the most influential Protestant body is the Methodist church. It is divided into the Northern and Southern churches and at a recent conference of the Southern church a motion to unite with the Northern church was voted down. The Roman Catholic church of Canada would strongly oppose annexation to the United States on account of the loose divorce laws of the Americans if there were no other reason.

Members of the legal and medical professions would oppose annexation because those

professions have a higher standing in Canada
than in the states. The examinations are more
severe in Canada and no quackery is tolerated.
The Canadian Pacific Railway Company would
oppose annexation because the line runs east
and west, connecting the provinces, and the
traffic will be much greater if the provinces
trade with one another than if they trade with
the states to the south.

To fully understand the situation one must
know something of the politics of Canada.
there are two parties known as Conservatives
and Reformers. The names are inappropriate.
they are relics of a past age and furnish no clue
to the politics of the parties which they represent. The names " National " and " Provincial " should be substituted for Conservative
and Reform. The Conservatives of Canada
very closely resemble the Republicans of the
United States, while the Reformers advocate
much the same principles as the American
Democrats. The Republicans of the United
States are pronounced protectionists ; so are
Canadian Conservatives. Both Democrats and
Reformers are, to use a word coined by the
Montreal *Witness*, " freetraprodectionists. '
They believe in free trade ; they talk about

the evils of protection ; but they assure the
manufacturers that they would not destroy the
protective character of the tariff if they had
the power. According to Republican principles the welfare of the republic should be
considered before that of the state. The
Democrats have always insisted upon the
preservation of state rights. The general
policy of the Conservative party is based upon
the belief that where the interests of any one
of the provinces in any matter conflict with
those of the country at large the province
should give way to the Dominion. They say
the whole is greater than its part. Conservatives look at public measures from a Dominion standpoint. Reformers look at them
from a provincial standpoint. In case of a
struggle between the province in which he
lived and Canada at large the sympathies of
the Conservative would be with the Dominion. The sympathies of the Reformer would
be with his province. The Conservatives
have always been more less disposed to
abolish provincial legislatures and have only
one great national parliament. If a Conservative in the legislature of any province
shows marked ability he is taken into the

circle of Dominion politics as soon as possible. The Reformers on the other hand make the most of the provincial legislatures and some of their ablest men are to be found in them. This is the reason why Reformers have generally controlled the local legislatures while the Conservatives have been in power at Ottawa. The Reformers instead of advocating legislative union and the abolition of the local legislatures favor a great extension of the powers of the provincial legislatures and even assert that the provinces would never have confederated had the people understood that the British North America Act so restricted the powers of the local legislatures. The Conservatives contend that while the policy of Canada may for a time be injurious to one province, that policy which most advances the country at large will in the end prove most advantageous to every section of it. This is the principle upon which the "National Policy" or protective tariff is based. Conservatives are willing to admit that in some cases it would be better for certain sections if certain duties were removed, but they say that if this principle of looking at everything from a sectional standpoint were adopted the tariff would have to be entirely abolished, for one section would object to one item and another to another. The policy of the Conservative or " National " party is to build up inter-provincial trade—to force the provinces to trade with one another instead of with the adjoining states. The Reformers say it makes little difference whether the provinces trade with one another or with the states so long as the trade is profitable. They tell the people of the maritime provinces that their natural market is in the eastern states. They advise the people of Ontario to trade with the adjoining states instead of with the eastern provinces and the Canadian North-West. They tell the people of the North-West that their natural market is in the western states and that they should resist any attempt to force trade into artificial channels. The policy of the Reform leaders, carried out, would probably lead to annexation but it does not follow that the body of the party would favor annexation. The great mass of voters would go over to the " Nationals " if they thought that the policy of the " Provincials " would result in that way. As it is the Conservative or " National " party has been kept in power at Ottawa almost constantly since confedera-

tion. It is the national sentiment of the
Conservatives that makes them advocate the
rapid construction of the Canadian Pacific
Railway in order that the country may from
ocean to ocean be bound together by bands of
steel ; it is the provincialism of the Reformers
that makes them oppose it. And so it is with
almost every question in Dominion and provincial politics. Many measures of course are
the result of pure partyism, but the distinguish-
ing characteristic of the Conservative party is
nationalism, while that of the Reform party
is provincialism.

Mr. Smith says the debt of Canada has
been doubled while that of the United States
has been reduced. The comparison is unfair.
The system of taxation in the two countries is
entirely different. There is no direct taxation
in Canada except for municipal purposes, the
cost of provincial government being paid out
of the Dominion treasury. In the United
States the cost of state government is paid by
direct taxation and many important public
works, which in Canada would be constructed
by the Dominion government are there under-
taken by the state governments. The whole
cost of government, Dominion and provincial,

in Canada is paid by indirect taxation in the shape of customs and excise duties. In the United States the tariff and excise duties are higher than in Canada, but the whole revenue from them is devoted to federal purposes. At present the states are much more densely populated than Canada, but the percentage of increase in population is greater in Canada. With increase in population there will be no corresponding increase in expenditure, for it costs very little more to administer the affairs of a densely populated country than those of a sparsely settled one of the same area. For example, Canada has more postoffices in proportion to population than any other country. The expenditure in that department will not increase in proportion to the increase of population. Canadians are just now engaged in the construction of most stupendous public works. The more costly of these will be completed in a few years, and it is safe to say that when Canada has a population of fifty million people the public debt will not be nearly so large per head of population as it is to-day.

Mr. Smith says the opening up of North West Canada will be a source of weakness rather than of strength. He will surely admit that anything that tends to develop national sentiment will strengthen the union of the provinces. The opening up of the North-West territory has enlarged the ideas of Canadians. They know that they have a great country and they are becoming proud of it. Nothing tends more to develop national sentiment than national pride. There is another reason why Canadians now have more national pride than formerly. Canada has always had a liberal school system, but until some time after confederation most of the text books were imported from the United States. They taught that the United States formed the greatest country under the sun, and that Canada was poor and insignificant. Every part of the United States was described in glowing terms, only one or two pages being devoted to Canada. Now the children in our schools, which are the best in the world, study from Canadian books, and learning that the country in which they live has wonderful resources, are proud to call themselves Canadians. The development of Canadian sentiment is seen not alone in Canada, but also in the United States. Canadians emigrating to that country at one time forgot so soon as possible that they were born in Canada and called themselves Americans. Now there are Canadian clubs in almost every large city in the Union. This feeling must in time result in the repatriation of thousands of Canadian-Americans.

Some people suppose that the Americans have a great advantage over Canadians in the possession of the southern states, but it seems to me that the people of a country where there is but one climate are more likely to remain a united nation than those of a country with such a variety of climates as the United States. It is well known that the character of a people is partly determined by climate, and the people of a country like Canada where there is very little variation in climate, are much more likely to ultimately form a homeogeneous nation than are those of a country like the United States. There has been so much migration in the United States owing to the opening up of new regions for settlement that the effect of climate is not so apparent as it would otherwise be. The population of the United States will probably always be migratory, but when the West and South are as populous as the East the movement will not be so general as at present. Excluding the southern states, Canadians have a very much larger area of habitable land than their neighbors. The people of the northern states, living in a climate similar to that of Canada, have given to the American nation its characteristic push and enterprise. The people of the South are comparatively indolent and unprogressive. The masses, composed of blacks and white "trash," are unable to either read or write, and the aristocratic classes still cling to seventeenth century ideas. Dueling is common throughout the South. Indeed, a large proportion of the people south of Mason and Dixon's line believe a resort to the code to be the proper means of obtaining redress for insult or injury. A short time ago Judge Reid, of Kentucky, was challenged by a lawyer whom he had offended. He declined to fight, believing dueling to be wrong, and was in consequence shunned by his friends and taunted with cowardice by his enemies until he was driven to suicide. There is no respect for the law in those states. Every man's hand is on his pistol pocket, and there is no regard for life. The courts are held in disrepute and lynchings occur almost every day. It is true that the cities of the South are making great progress industrially. With cheap labor and raw material close at hand they are likely to crowd the Northerners out of the market in many branches of industry, or else bring about a reduction of wages in the North. Mere industrial activity, however, does not necessarily make a prosperous people. An ignorant people can not be truly prosperous, and the people of the South are very ignorant. In 1876 there were in the United States 5,658,144 people over the age of fourteen who could neither read nor write. In 1880 there were 6,239,958. In most of the northern states there was a slight decrease in illiteracy during that decade, but in the South illiteracy greatly increased, there being 551,201 more illiterates in the South in 1880 than there were in 1870. The illiterate negroes of the United States outnumber the illiterate whites, but there are over three million whites over the age of fourteen who can neither read nor write.

It is said that the people of Jamaica will soon ask for admission to the Dominion of Canada. The proposition should not be entertained by Canadians. The population is very like that of the southern states, and the climate is such that the people can never become Canadians. The population is 580,800, of which 444,186 are negroes. We don't want any black men in the Canadian Parliament. But Jamaica and other British possessions in the West Indies, which have altogether a territory of nearly fourteen thousand square miles and a population of about one and a quarter millions, might join a Canadian zollverein. A political union of all the colonies would be impracticable, but a commercial union is quite practicable, and by means of it Jamaica would secure all the advantages of annexation to Canada with none of its disadvantages. If Jamaica were a regular province of Canada disputes would certainly arise between the Dominion and provincial governments that might cause most serious trouble, but if free trade could be established between the two countries, each remaining politically independent of the other, it would give a great impetus to the trade of both.

There will be trouble in the western states as well as in the southern states. A great oligarchy is establishing itself within the Republic and is growing stronger every day. The people at large are opposed to Mormonism, but they seem unable to cope with it. The Mormons are already well established in Utah. and they are extending their influence through the west. More than two thousand Utah Mormons are said to have settled in Idaho within the past year. They are numerous in Arizona, Montana and Nevada, and have missionaries everywhere in the South where the ignorant people are easily persuaded to join the church. The public opinion of the United States is very much opposed to the Mormons, but they hope to withstand it until they are numerous enough to make a bargain with one of the political parties and secure representation in the electoral college, when they will become so influential that they cannot be dislodged without bloodshed.

I do not take a pessimistic view of the future of the United States. The people are wonderfully enterprising and very hopeful. They believe in themselves and in their country, and the national sentiment is strong enough throughout the union to overcome many difficulties, but Canadians have enough to do to rectify their own mistakes and bear their own burdens without shouldering the burdens of the Americans. It seems to me strange that one who considers the French population of Canada an insuperable obstacle to the consolidation of the country can overlook the color line, Mormonism and the differences of climate in the United States.

Many people have wondered why Mr. Goldwin Smith, who has so little confidence in the future of Canada, has made it his home. The explanation is simple. Mr. Smith is a pessimist. Not feeling at home in England he emigrated to the United States. But the people of that country were too hopeful. They are a sensible people and refuse to look on the dark side of things; Mr. Smith was out of place there. Coming to Canada he found thousands of people who were ready to agree with him. There are probably more pessimists in Canada in proportion to population than in any other country. These pessimists form a minority of the people, but they are numerous enough to make a great deal of noise. They refuse to believe anything good of Canada. They belittle the resources of the Dominion, and declare that it can never be anything more than an agricultural country and that farming doesn't pay. If five million people do not accomplish quite so much as fifty million the pessimists declare that the country is unprogressive and the people unenterprising, but when those five million people undertake the construction of great national works and carry them to completion with unexampled rapidity, they say they were constructed too fast and that the people will be ruined in consequence. If a factory closes they proclaim it on the housetops ; if a new factory is started they close their eyes and pass by. If the immigration is large they say most of the immigrants are paupers. If there is a decrease in immigration during the year they are sure the population is stationary. If a Canadian secures a good position in the United States, they say the country is being depleted of its population and that the United States is being built up by the exodus. If an American accepts a good position in Canada they complain that all the best positions are being filled by foreigners. So long as men are imperfect legislatures will make mistakes. The representatives of the people will sometimes allow sectional prejudices and local jealousies to overshadow the general welfare. They will sometimes make corrupt bargains and work to advance their own interests at the expense of the people whom they represent. This happens in every country. When it happens in Canada the pessimists declare that Confederation is a failure. The pessimist always believes that his province is paying the whole cost of carrying on the government of the country. If he lives in Ontario, he says Ontario is the milch cow of the Confederation and that all the other provinces are living at its expense. If this were true the other provinces would have great cause for rejoicing, but the same pessimist migrating to another province is prepared to swear that it pays more money into the Dominion treasury in proportion to population than any other province.

It is very different in the United States. There the people unite in praising the country and its institutions, and will not suffer anyone to belittle them. Said an American visitor to Toronto recently, " If some of your leading newspapers were in the United States they would have been burned out long ago. The people wouldn't let them cry down the enterprises of the country and destroy its credit at home and abroad. A few matches, a piece of hemp and a lamp post would settle the business for them." There are men who cannot succeed in any country. Inability, indolence, rash speculation, or bad luck always keep them back. Such men are committing suicide in the United

States every day, and no one ascribes their failure to the country. But in Canada if a man's expectations are not fully realized, he and all his friends insist that the country is to blame, that no one can succeed in Canada. If they would read the labor statistics published by the Ontario government they would find that the average of wages in the Province of Ontario is higher than in the city of Chicago.

But the noisy pessimists are in the minority, and as the country grows in population and in wealth they will almost entirely disappear. The pessimists are very fond of saying that Canada has length without breadth, that it is like a fishing pole extending from the Atlantic to the Pacific. Well, each end of the fishing pole has a line in the finest fisheries of the whole world. It is sometimes said that the habitable part of Canada is about three thousand miles long and one hundred wide. This statement is made only by those who have never gone on exploring expeditions themselves, and will not believe the reports of those who have done so. The settled part of Canada is only about one hundred miles wide on the average, but the surveyors who have carefully explored the country, examined the soil and observed the climate say the habitable part of Canada is at least five hundred miles wide on the average. About one hundred miles north of the great lakes is a belt of rocky country, the greater part of which is of little value for agricultural purposes ; but there are rich mines, vast areas of timber and valuable fisheries, and grasses grow with such luxuriance that it must become some day one of the greatest stock-raising countries in the world. This region extends northward to the height of land, the water-shed separating the waters flowing into the great lakes from those flowing into Hudson Bay. On the other side of the height of land a fertile, well-wooded country slopes down to the Hudson Bay. The rivers all rise in the neighborhood of the rocky section. If it were as smooth and fertile as other parts of the country it would soon be stripped of timber near the sources of the rivers, and the country would be subject to floods such as those which have devastated Ohio and other sections of the United States owing to the destruction of forests. But the Ontario government, having wisely recognized the necessity of preserving the forests, can easily keep that region at the sources of the rivers always well-timbered. The mines and the fisheries can be developed, lumbering can be carried on under the supervision of a government forestry bureau, and stock raisers can avail themselves of the succulent grasses. North of that narrow strip are millions of acres of fertile farm lands. The country between the height of land and Hudson Bay only requires a railway to develop it, and a railway has already been chartered. The Nipissing and James Bay railway, chartered by the Dominion Parliament in April, 1884, will extend from near Callandar on the line of the Canadian Pacific railway to James Bay, the southern prolongation of Hudson Bay, through a country well adapted for farming, grazing and dairy purposes. According to the reports of Professor Bell and other well known scientists there are immense deposits of iron and anthracite coal side by side along the rivers emptying into James Bay. The distance from Toronto to James Bay via the Northern, Pacific Junction and James Bay railways will be 575 miles. When the railway to James Bay is completed anthracite coal will be brought from the northern mines to the people of southern Ontario. Near the City of Ottawa is a mountain of the finest iron in the world. The coal mines of the James Bay region will be connected by railway with Ottawa, and also with the rich iron mines on the north shore of Lake Superior, less than 300 miles away. South of the anthracite coal region are enormous beds of lignite coal, peat and porcelain or china clay of superior quality. Of course

many people in southern Ontario will say that all
this fertile land, timber, coal, iron and other minerals must go to waste because the country is too
cold. That is because they have never lived in
the country. People living in the United States
not very far south of the great lakes have much
the same opinion of southern Ontario, but those
who have lived in both countries or have studied
the reports of the government observatories know
that the climate of southern Ontario is more mod-
erate than that of many of the states farther south.
The winters are longer and steadier, but there are
not such extremes of either heat or cold. So it is
with northern Ontario. It is colder than southern
Ontario, but not so cold as the section near the
height of land. Scientists who have lived north of
the height of land and made careful observations,
say that the climate moderates as the descent
towards James Bay is made. This is due partly to
the lower elevation and partly to the proximity of
a large body of open water. The country lies
between the great lakes and the Hudson bay, and
large bodies of open water always modify the climate of the surrounding country. It must not be
supposed that there is any doubt about the navi-
gability of Hudson bay. The bay is always open,
but the straits at the far north are sometimes ob-

structed by ice, and it is doubtful whether they are open long enough to make the Hudson Bay route to Europe profitable. There is no doubt about the climate of the country to the south of James Bay. The following report of the temperature at Moose Factory on the shore of James Bay is taken from the report of the meteorological service of Canada for the year ending 31st December, 1881 :—

1881.	JAN.	FEB.	MAR.	APRIL	MAY	JUNE	JULY	AUG.	SEPT.	OCT.	NOV.	DEC.
Mean temp.	10·6	6·9	16·1	22·6	48·2	47·4	64·0	60·8	51·5	32·6	12·3	3·0
Highest do.	20·1	36·1	44·2	56·8	79·0	83·0	90·5	88·5	76·8	71·2	52·0	37·1
Lowest do.	39·6	34·5	14·3	17·9	14·0	26·8	41·5	38·2	35·0	12·5	29·1	22·2

So much for that part of Canada lying north of the height of land. It is well known that the most fertile part of the Canadian North-West lies some distance north of the Canadian Pacific railway and there is no doubt that the railway runs through a very fertile country. Canada has breadth as well as length. It is not as broad as it is long and it is well that it is so. Those who say that it would be better for Canada if it could be doubled up show their ignorance of history. The movement of population is always more rapid along the parallels of latitude than along the parallels of longitude. One can follow the parallels of latitude a long way without noticing any change in climate, but along the parallels of longitude the climate varies greatly. The effect of the difference in longitude on climate is sometimes counteracted by difference in elevation or the presence of large bodies of water, but in a vast country as broad as it is long there must be greater differences in climate than in the same area lengthened out. Accordingly the people of Canada extending along a few parallels of latitude from the Atlantic to the Pacific, are more likely to form a homeogeneous nation than if habitable Canada were as broad as it is long.

Canadians who would rather brag than grumble can easily find something to talk about. All Canada lies north of the cyclone belt. It has been estimated that three-fourths of the land adapted to the production of wheat in North America lies within the Dominion of Canada. The richest iron deposits on the continent belong to Canada, and it can supply the whole world with fish.

Canadian pessimists talk about the wonderful increase of the population of the United States. Well, the population of the provinces which now form the Dominion of Canada has doubled eighteen times since 1790, while that of the United

States has doubled twelve and a half times in the same period. It may be said that this is an unfair comparison, but a comparison of Canada's progress since Confederation with the progress of the United States during the first seventeen years after the Declaration of Independence would be still more favorable to Canada. Because the country south of the boundary line is more densely populated many people foolishly suppose that if the provinces had been annexed to the United States the country would have been densely settled long ago. But Dakota and Montana are in the United States, and yet the great American desert was settled up before the fertile lands of Dakota and Montana were invaded by the white man. Migration follows the parallels of latitude. If the Canadian North-West were in the United States it would still be known as the Great Lone Land. There would be no railways and no settlers there. Just as Dakota and Montana remained in the possession of the Indians until the less fertile land to the south was peopled, so the Hudson Bay Territory would have been left to the Indians and buffalo until Dakota and Montana were peopled. After the lands of Dakota and Montana were nearly all taken up by settlers or grabbed by monopolists, the migrants would begin to go farther

north. Manitoba and the North-West territories
of Canada are at least a decade ahead on account
of being within the Dominion of Canada. When
Dakota and Montana are well settled the boundary
line will not stop the tide of emigration. The
first to cross the boundary line into Canada will
be thousands of Canadians who have taken up
land in Dakota. In a few years many Canadian-
Americans will sell their lands and take up free
grants in the Canadian North-West. They will
be followed by thousands of Americans.

The Canadian provinces have made great progress in the past; they will make wonderful progress in the future. Canada has the best geographical position for commercial purposes of any
country in the world. Lying between Europe and
Asia, it is the shortest route for the commerce of
the world. On its Atlantic and Pacific coasts are
the finest harbors in America; close to them are
immense deposits of coal. The long stretch of the
United States coast line is almost destitute of coal.
Ocean vessels from Europe passing up the St. Lawrence to Montreal can go farther inland than by
any United States route, and far inland as it is,
Montreal is 200 miles nearer Liverpool than New
York is. But sea-sick people need not travel as
far as Montreal by water. Louisburg, Canada's

most eastern port, which has one of the grandest harbors in the world, is 750 nautical miles nearer to England than New York, so that while ocean vessels can go farther inland by the Canadian route than by any other, Canadian railway trains can approach much nearer to Europe than those of the United States. The Pacific ports of Canada are much nearer Asia than those of the United States, and the Japan current carries all vessels bound from Asia to America toward Canada, so that vessels bound for San Francisco must go many hundreds of miles out of their way. Moreover there are easier grades all along the line of the Canadian Pacific railway than by any American route. The Rocky Mountains are only 3,646 feet above the level of the ocean at the highest point of the C. P. R. The United States railways rise to the height of a mile and a half, and the Union Pacific for 1,300 miles runs at a higher elevation than the highest point of the Canadian railway. If the navigation of Hudson straits proves practicable, Japan will be over 2,300 miles nearer Liverpool by the Canadian Pacific and Hudson Bay railways than by any American route.

Not only has Canada the advantage of the United States in being nearer to Europe and Asia and being especially favored by the Japan current, but the internal water system of Canada is far superior to that of the United States. The great lakes lie between the two countries, but the connecting links are in Canada. When the Trent Valley canal connecting the Georgian Bay with Lake Ontario is completed, all the long voyage by Lakes Huron, St. Clair, Erie and Ontario will be saved. There is very little cutting to be done, for there is natural water communication by the Trent river nearly all the way and it will cost very little to complete the work already commenced of constructing a barge canal. The cost of making a ship canal would not be enormous and that will probably be done some day. There is also water communication nearly all the way between the Georgian bay and the great Ottawa river, and for less than the cost of the Welland canal improvements can be made, which will enable Lake Superior steamers to take a short cut to Montreal via the Ottawa river.

Canada now occupies the position of the fourth maritime state in the world. It has, as the Ottawa *Free Press* recently pointed out, a population equal to that of England in Queen Elizabeth's reign and a commerce equal to that of England at the beginning of the present century. If Canadians take advantage of the commanding geographical position of their country they will be the greatest commercial nation in the world one hundred years from now. Canada will never, in all probability, have as large a population as the United States, although it will within one hundred years have a much larger population than that country has to-day. But Canada throughout its vast extent has an invigorating climate, the people are nearly all of Caucasian origin, the standard of education is high, and while it will be very many years before the various nationalities are merged into one, the influences of climate and association will all tend in that direction.

www.ingramcontent.com/pod-product-compliance
Lightning Source LLC
Chambersburg PA
CBHW020327090426
42735CB00009B/1441